British Airships in Pictures

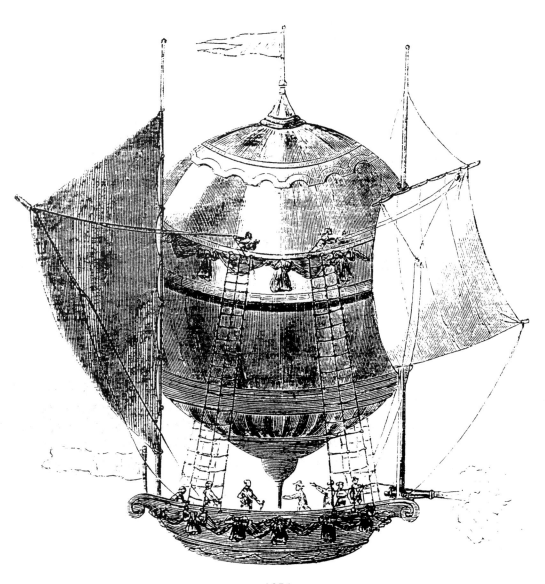

1856

British Airships in Pictures

An illustrated history 1784–1998

PATRICK ABBOTT AND NICK WALMSLEY

No. 9 was the first British rigid airship to fly. See numbers 57–59 (pages 58–60).

Frontispiece: The trail rope of a Coastal airship passes under the pulley wheel of a 'snatch block', so enabling the landing party to pull her down without being lifted off their feet. See number 43 (pages 44–5).

Opposite: R.34 in America. Cylinders of hydrogen are stacked in the foreground and an airman waves from the top gun platform. See numbers 74–78 (pages 75–9).

British Cataloguing in Publication Data
A catalogue record for this book
is available from the British Library

ISBN 1 899863 48 6

First published by House of Lochar 1998

© Patrick Abbott and Nick Walmsley

Printed in Great Britain by
Redwood Books, Trowbridge
for House of Lochar, Isle of Colonsay,
Argyll PA61 7YR

Also by Patrick Abbott
Family Patterns
Airship: the story of R.34
The British Airship at War 1914–1918
Airships (Shire Publications)

Contents

Introduction 7

Theory and Fantasy: 1784–1901 9
Experimentation and Achievement: 1902–1913 15
War and Service: 1914–1918 27
Triumph and Tragedy: 1919–1930 73
Demise and Renaissance: 1931–1998 93

Provisional list of viable British airships 109
Bibliography 111
Acknowledgements 112

The Willows airship No.4, which became Naval Airship No.2. See number 15 (page 19).

A Coastal airship leaves the hangar on a windy day. See numbers 44–48 (pages 46–50).

Introduction

Airships, sometimes known as 'dirigibles', are aircraft which are propelled by engines, but which float in the air because of the lift of a buoyant gas. Hydrogen, which is inflammable, was used at first, as it is cheap and readily available, but helium, which does not burn, is preferred nowadays, despite being slightly heavier and more expensive. Coal gas was also used occasionally in the early days, and some small, modern airships use hot air.

To be efficient, airships need to be not only streamlined and light, but also as large as possible, in order to combine the maximum volume and lift with the minimum surface area and drag. To comply with these requirements, three types of normal airship have been evolved: the 'non-rigid', the 'semi-rigid' and the 'rigid'.

A typical non-rigid, or 'blimp', consists of a fabric gasbag or 'envelope' beneath which, supported by rigging, is a 'car' or 'gondola', containing the engine and crew compartment. When helium is used, the car may be safely fastened tight against the envelope, with the rigging lines placed inside. The envelope is kept firm and taut by means of internal bags, called 'ballonets', into which air is directed as required, to maintain pressure. The first successful non-rigids were made in France by a Brazilian, Alberto Santos-Dumont, at the end of the nineteenth century. Non-rigids have been made and flown up to the present day.

Although usually much larger, a semi-rigid is basically the same as a non-rigid, but has an envelope additionally stiffened by a long metal keel stretching internally from bow to stern. The rigging lines may be internal and the cars attached directly to the keel. The first successful semi-rigid was built in 1902 in France, by the Lebaudy brothers. Later examples came also from Italy and Russia, but no true semi-rigids have been made anywhere since the nineteen thirties, although a small Lebaudy replica was built in 1967 for a film.

A rigid is the largest of all types of airship and has a 'hull' consisting of a lightweight framework of girders covered by fabric, inside which are several separate gasbags, tailored to fill all the available space. No matter how much gas is released, the airship retains its streamlined form and provides a firm attachment for the stabilising fins and other features. The engines are usually in cars suspended below the hull, but accommodation and storage space can be provided inside. The rigid airship was invented by Count Ferdinand von Zeppelin of Germany in the opening years of this century. They were subsequently made also by Britain, France and the United States, but no conventional rigid airship or 'zeppelin' has been built anywhere since before the Second World War.

All airships of whatever type have similar properties, however. Static lift is derived from the weight of air displaced, less the weight of the gas displacing it. At sea level, each 32,000 cubic feet of air weighs about 1.07 tons, while a similar volume of hydrogen weighs 0.07 tons, so producing a lift of around 1.0 ton. Helium is twice as heavy as hydrogen, so the same volume produces around 0.93 tons of lift. From the 'gross lift' of the gas is deducted the weight of the airship's structure and permanent fittings to give the amount of 'useful lift' or 'disposable lift' available for fuel, ballast, crew, cargo and passengers. When ballast – usually water – is released, an airship becomes lighter and ascends; when gas is released, it becomes heavier and descends. In theory, an airship should be flown in a state of neutral buoyancy, neither heavy nor light, and it can then climb or dive by an alteration of attitude. In practice, however, the conditions of lift change continuously, as the pressure and temperature of the gas and of the surrounding air alter. Atmospheric pressure decreases with altitude, so as an airship climbs, the hydrogen inside expands while the air outside similarly becomes thinner. The rate of ascent thus remains constant, until the 'pressure height' is reached, when no further expansion within the gasbags is possible and the gas is forced out through automatic valves. The rate of climb then slackens until, at the airship's 'ceiling', it ceases entirely. If the ambient air becomes colder than the enclosed gas, or if sunshine causes the gas to become hotter than the air, this causes 'superheating' and a temporary increase in buoyancy known as 'false lift'. The opposite effect of 'supercooling' can also occur – usually at night – when the gas becomes colder than the air and there is 'latent lift', as some buoyancy is lost for a time. But although these fluctuations are always present to some extent, it is not necessary to be constantly controlling them by the release of ballast or gas, for there is an additional method of varying the lift. If an airship is flown in a nose-up attitude, then not only is the thrust line of the propellers inclined, but the hull or envelope acts like an aeroplane's wing and gives 'dynamic lift', which supplements the 'static lift' of the gas. With a tail-up attitude, the same effect can also be applied downward instead of upward, and the use of these forces enables an airship to fly at the desired height for long periods without needlessly wasting gas or ballast. To control the ship's attitude in this way, 'elevators' or horizontal rudders, which raise or depress the tail, are normally employed. In addition, the 'trim' can be changed by moving the centres of lift or gravity in some way and so tilting the airship . A few airships have had propellers which swivel to push the vessel up or down.

Because of the necessity to be both light and large, all airships are at once fragile and cumbersome, requiring a large ground crew when being handled and enormous hangars for construction, shelter or maintenance. They are also very slow. However, they are usually quiet, reliable, economical, possessed of great endurance and capable of providing spacious accommodation. Nowadays they are also much safer than is commonly believed, for the notorious airship disasters of the early twentieth century were caused by inadequate weather forecasting, bad design or the lack of helium: all factors which no longer apply. And the only paying passengers ever to have been killed in an airship accident were the thirteen who died in the *Hindenburg* disaster of 1937.

Britain eventually built more non-rigids than any other country except the United States, and more rigids than any other country except Germany. In recent years, our airship designers have led the world.

This time, the ballonets could not cope with the conditions. See numbers 26–27 (page 29).

Theory and Fantasy
1784–1901

The first successful balloons were made in France in 1783 and designs for dirigibles appeared soon afterwards. But because no power source was available that was both light and strong, no really practicable airships appeared anywhere before the end of the nineteenth century. However, in 1852 Henri Giffard of France achieved a small measure of success with a steam-powered dirigible and in 1884 Renard and Krebs built an airship powered by electricity which made the world's first circular flight. Other countries achieved little and although in Britain, as elsewhere, many strange and ingenious aircraft were built, planned or suggested, all were doomed to failure.

I. Vincent Lunardi, a Neapolitan resident in London, made the first balloon flight in England, on 15 September 1784, when he flew from the Artillery Ground at Moorfield and made a final landing at Standon, near Ware in Hertfordshire, just over two hours later. Because he attempted to propel his craft with oars, it could be said that he envisaged it as a dirigible, but as it was the wrong shape, used an ineffectual method of propulsion and possessed no power source stronger than human muscles, the journey can in no way be claimed as controlled flight.

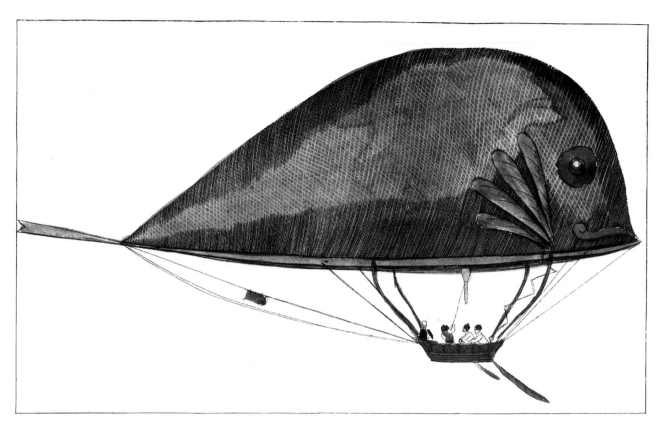

2. The first dirigible balloon of streamlined form to appear in this country was the *Dolphin*, which Durs Egg and John Pauly, two Swiss residents of London, started to build in 1816. It was virtually a semi-rigid , for the envelope, which incorporated a ballonet, was braced by a ventral frame, from which the car was suspended. Slung between the car and the tail was a barrel of water which could be moved to control the trim, or its contents released as ballast. Propulsion was to be by oars and by flappers intended to provide thrust by pushing the air backwards. Even had the project not been abandoned before completion, the lack of a suitable engine would have proved fatal to success.

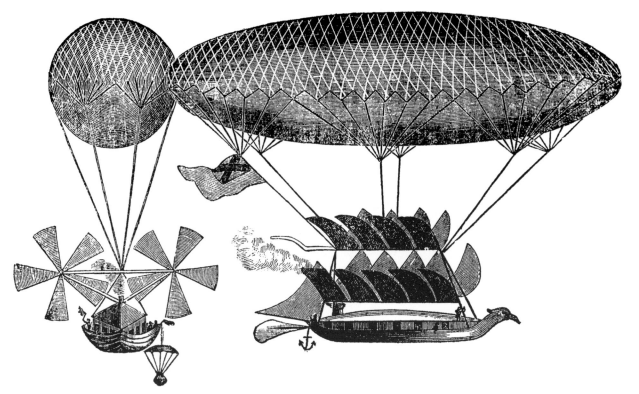

3. Sir George Cayley, the famous aeroplane pioneer, also drew up designs for a steam-powered airship in 1817. There were two alternative versions: one propelled by airscrews and the other by flappers. Although neither form was ever constructed, there were some farsighted features, including the provision of a parachute. This appears to be the first time such an apparatus was visualised as an adjunct to safety rather than merely a device for public entertainment.

4. Little beyond a tantalising drawing is known of the obscure airship designed by one J.M. Partridge in 1847. He called his creation a 'pneumadrome' and it incorporated some advanced features. Light netting covered the envelope, which was of canvas treated with rubber and supported internally by a light trussed framework of rings and longitudinal bars, so making the craft a type of semi-rigid or rigid airship. Despite this, a ballonet was also fitted, to maintain internal pressure, and this was controlled by a valve and a pump. Three pusher propellers were provided, and two large stern sails were fitted, to give extra lift. Together with a small head sail, these were provided with braces and halliards and so could also be manipulated for steering. Although no suitable engine was available to the inventor, it is alleged that he completed the aircraft and even flew it more than once in some uncontrolled manner.

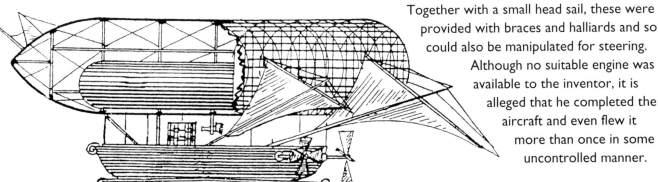

5. The *Locomotive Balloon* was designed and built by Hugh Bell. The envelope, which was 50ft long and had a capacity of 15,000ft³, was made of silk and inflated with coal gas. This was the first verified occasion that an airscrew was used on a British aircraft, but as it was operated manually, its effect was negligible. The balloon ascended from the Vauxhall Gardens in May 1850, but simply drifted with the wind for several miles before descending.

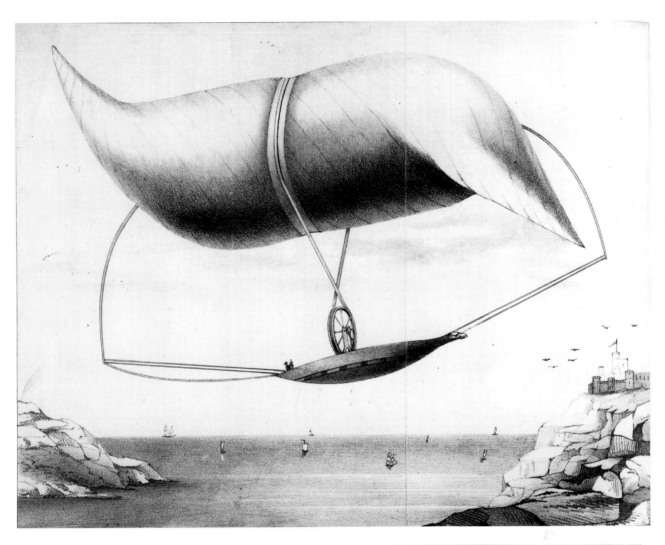

6. This extraordinary device, designed by John Luntley, was never constructed, although a model was shown at the Great Exhibition of 1851. The intention was to provide an elongated and spiral-shaped envelope, which would rotate round a horizontal metal axle and so act as its own propeller. It would be turned by an endless belt from a steam-driven pulley wheel in the car below. A ballonet was planned, to keep the envelope in shape, and the trim was to be controlled by moving the car forwards or backwards. The hollow axle was intended to duct steam from the engine through the envelope, so both condensing the steam and warming the gas to keep it fully expanded.

JUST PUBLISHED,

Price 1s. 6d., with a Lithographic View.

AIR NAVIGATION,

BY THE

ROTARY BALLOON.

Provisionally Registered, 26th April 1851.

By J. LUNTLEY.

This Publication is intended to develop the idea put forth in the model at the *Great Exhibition*, Class X, No. 237; and contains a sketch of the history of Aerostation to the present time.

> " Soon shall thy arm, unconquered Steam ! afar
> Drag the slow barge, or drive the rapid car;
> Or, on wide-waving wings expanded, bear
> The flying chariot through the fields of air."
> DARWIN's *Botanic Garden*, 290.

LONDON:

HOULSTON & STONEMAN, 65, Paternoster Row; And all Booksellers.

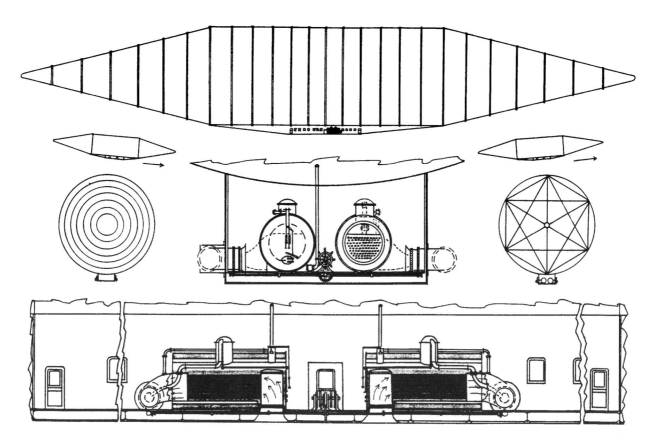

7. In 1866, Richard Boyman drew up plans for an all-metal rigid airship with a steel hull of geometrical shape, supported by internal hoops. The length of this enormous 'aerial ship' was calculated at a precise 1,302·893ft – very nearly a quarter of a mile! It was intended to be propelled by jets of steam, issuing through nozzles that could also be swivelled to push the airship upwards or downwards. Weighing some six hundred tons fully equipped, it was to have been kept aloft by the lift of nearly 20 millionft^3 of hydrogen, although the inventor confidently hoped that 'a more buoyant gas will be discovered', so allowing the vessel's size to be reduced!

Experimentation and Achievement 1902–1913

With the invention of the internal combustion engine, towards the end of the nineteenth century, a lightweight power source at last became available. In France, the first practicable non-rigid airships were built by a Brazilian, Alberto Santos-Dumont, and the first semi-rigid by the Lebaudy brothers. In Germany, the first successful rigid airships soon appeared, designed and built by Count Ferdinand von Zeppelin. Inventors in other countries followed suit and although England entered the field belatedly, considerable progress was made in the years leading up to the First World War.

8. The airship built by a well-known balloonist, Stanley Spencer, in 1902, was only 75ft long and 20ft in diameter, with a capacity of 20,000ft^3. This was the first British dirigible actually to make some form of controlled flight, but it was powered by only a small Simms petrol engine, driving a single propeller at a very slow speed, and it could not make headway against even a slight wind. On 22 September, carrying only the inventor in the small basketwork car, it ascended from Crystal Palace, and drifted westwards before landing safely nearly two hours later at Eastcote, near Ruislip.

9. The non-rigid airship built by Dr. F.A. Barton, assisted by F.L. Rawson, was 180ft long, 40ft in diameter, with a capacity of 200,000ft^3. It had a car made of bamboo, 127ft long and 18ft high, on which was fitted a deck carrying two 50hp Buchet engines, each driving two propellers. These failed to deliver sufficient power and the airship was pushed mostly by the wind during its only flight, on 22 July 1905, when it flew from Alexandra Palace to Romford in Essex. The dirigible was destroyed on landing but the crew of six were unharmed.

11. The *Nulli Secundus* ('Second to none') was the first military airship built in England. It was 122ft long, with a diameter of 26ft and a capacity of 55,000ft^3. On 5 October 1907, carrying Colonel John Capper and Samuel F. Cody, it flew from Farnborough to the centre of London, where it circled Trafalgar Square and the dome of St. Paul's before landing at the Crystal Palace, after covering some fifty miles in three and a half hours. Bad weather prevented a return flight and the airship had to be deflated and taken back by road to Farnborough.

10. The Willows airship No.1 was the first practicable airship in Britain, despite having no ballonet fitted. It was 72ft long, with a diameter of 18ft and had a capacity of 12,000ft^3. A Peugeot motor-cycle engine drove one propeller at the rear for propulsion and two swivelling propellers at the front for control. On 5 September 1905, taking off from Splott, near Cardiff, Ernest Willows flew successfully for over an hour.

12. In 1908, *Nulli Secundus* was rebuilt as a form of semi-rigid. It had a slightly increased capacity of 56,000ft^3 and an improved top speed of 22mph. It made several flights during the summer before being finally dismantled.

13. The car of *Nulli Secundus* carried the crew and a French eight-cylinder 50hp Antoinette engine, which drove two metal propellers.

14. The Willows No.2 was 86ft long, 22ft in diameter and had a capacity of 21,000ft^3. It was fitted with a ballonet, a rudder for steering and an eight-cylinder 35hp J.A.P. engine which drove twin swivelling propellers that provided both propulsion and vertical control. On 6–7 August 1910, it flew from Cardiff to London in less than 10 hours.

15. On 4 November 1910, the Willows No.3, developed from No.2 and named *City of Cardiff*, left Wormwood Scrubs to become the first British airship to cross the English Channel and the first airship to fly from England to France, arriving in the small hours of the following morning. After landing first at Douai, it then flew on to Paris, where Ernest Willows and his mechanic, Frank Goodden, became the first ever British aviators to fly into the French capital. The airship was 120ft long, 23ft in diameter and had a capacity of 32,000ft^3. Willows went on to make five airships in all, the fourth of which was bought by the Admiralty and became Naval Airship No.2. She appeared at the Spithead Naval Review in July 1914, but was used mainly for training purposes. Her spare envelope was later provided with an aeroplane fuselage as a car and became SS.1, the prototype for many wartime blimps.

16. Naval Airship No.1 was ordered by the Admiralty in 1909 and completed by Vickers, at Barrow-in-Furness, in 1911. She was the first rigid airship to be made in Britain and her framework was of duralumin. Her design was based on German Zeppelin practice but she was of the mathematically determined 'Zahm' shape, the radius of the bow outline being twice the diameter of the central parallel portion and the stern outline being nine times the diameter.

17. As Naval Airship No.1 never flew, she became popularly known as the 'Mayfly' and was finally scrapped after breaking in two when being taken out of her hangar on 24 September 1911. Powered by two 160hp Wolseley engines, she was 512ft long, with a diameter of 48ft and a total capacity of 664,000ft^3.

18. Army Airship No.3 or *Baby* was built in 1909 and powered first by two three-cylinder 8hp Buchet engines, turning one propeller, and then by a single 30hp seven-cylinder R.E.P. radial engine driving two propellers. It was only 84ft long, with a capacity of 21,000ft^3, and reached a speed of barely 20mph. As with several other early dirigibles, its envelope was made not of treated fabric, but of goldbeater's skins: the outer membrane of part of the large intestine of an ox.

19. In 1910, when the Army Balloon Factory rebuilt *Baby* extensively and renamed it *Beta*, it became the first really successful military airship in this country. It was subsequently rebuilt more than once, eventually reaching a length of 108ft and a capacity of 42,000ft^3. A 50hp Clerget engine drove two propellers and gave a quite creditable top speed of 35mph. Among other exploits, the airship was fitted experimentally with a machine-gun, took the Prince of Wales for a flight and became the first dirigible to carry lightweight radio equipment, or wireless telegraphy, as it was then known.

20. In February 1912, at Farnborough, *Beta* became the first non-rigid to be attached to a mooring mast. Two years later she was designated Naval Airship No.17, when the Admiralty took over all airships. She was used for reconnaissance work in Belgium during the early part of the First World War, and flew over night-time London to check the blackout. She was then relegated to training duties before being finally deleted from the active list in May 1916.

21. Seven Army airships were built in all, including the two versions of *Nulli Secundus*, *Baby* and *Beta*. The fifth, *Gamma* – shown here at the Farnborough mooring mast – was built in 1910 and rebuilt in 1912. She was powered by two 45hp Iris engines, which gave her a speed of about 30 m.p.h., and her envelope – of rubberized fabric – had a capacity of 101,000ft^3. Fitted with wireless telegraphy and commanded by Major Edward Maitland, she observed so effectively during the 1912 Army Manoeuvres that the exercises had to finish a day earlier than planned.

22. The last but one Army airship was *Delta*, built at the Army Aircraft Factory in 1912 but subsequently modified more than once. She had a capacity of 175,000ft^3 and was powered by two 110hp White and Poppe engines, driving a pair of swivelling propellers and giving her a top speed of 42mph. On 18 October 1913, Colonel Maitland jumped from *Delta* to make the world's first parachute descent from an airship. *Beta* can be seen in the background.

23. The last Army airship was *Eta*, delivered in 1913. She had a capacity of 118,000ft^3, carried a crew of five and was powered by two 80hp engines. She pioneered a new method of suspending the car, by attaching the rigging lines to D-shaped steel rings. Through these were passed cloth webbing pieces which were sewn and glued to the envelope with strengthening pieces of fabric. Each assembly consequently became known as an 'Eta patch' and they were afterwards used on many wartime airships. In January 1914, the four existing Army airships were taken over by the Admiralty but although flown operationally during the first months of the war, they were soon relegated to training duties. All four were eventually deleted from the active list in May 1916 and scrapped.

War and Service
1914–1918

The British military airships of the First World War were flown by the Airship Service, which was a branch of the Royal Naval Air Service until April 1918. The wartime British airships were conspicuously successful in countering the German submarine menace, protecting convoys and patrolling coastal waters. Only seven British airships were in commission in August 1914, when the war started, and of these, two had been bought from abroad. However, more than two hundred airships were built during the war, of which over a score were sold to the Allies and more than a hundred remained active at the Armistice. They were mostly small, cheap and hastily designed aircraft, but they were deployed with skill and not wasted on doomed bombing missions over enemy territory, as were the large, expensive and more sophisticated German zeppelins. British rigid airships came late on the scene and the total number of hours flown in wartime service by the eight rigids delivered before the Armistice was fewer than was flown individually by at least three small blimps, each of which cost a tiny fraction of the cost of one rigid. There is no recorded case of airships from the two sides meeting in direct combat.

24. When the threat of the German U-boats to British shipping became apparent, the Admiralty ordered construction of a fleet of small blimps, to be built as soon as possible. There were eventually three main types of these SS or 'Submarine Scout' airships, the first of which were built quickly and inexpensively by slinging the fuselage of a B.E.2c aeroplane beneath a simple envelope, using wire rigging and Eta patches. The envelope was 143ft long and of 60,000ft^3 capacity, made of rubberised cloth and fitted with two ballonets. Each airship was provided with bombs, wireless telegraphy and an extra fuel tank. They carried a pilot and a W/T (Wireless Telegraphy) operator and could remain aloft for up to 16 hours and reach a top speed of about 50mph. Like many later wartime blimps, they were assembled by the Airship Service at Kingsnorth on the Isle of Grain from components made elsewhere. Twenty-nine of this type were delivered, at a cost of some £2,500 each.

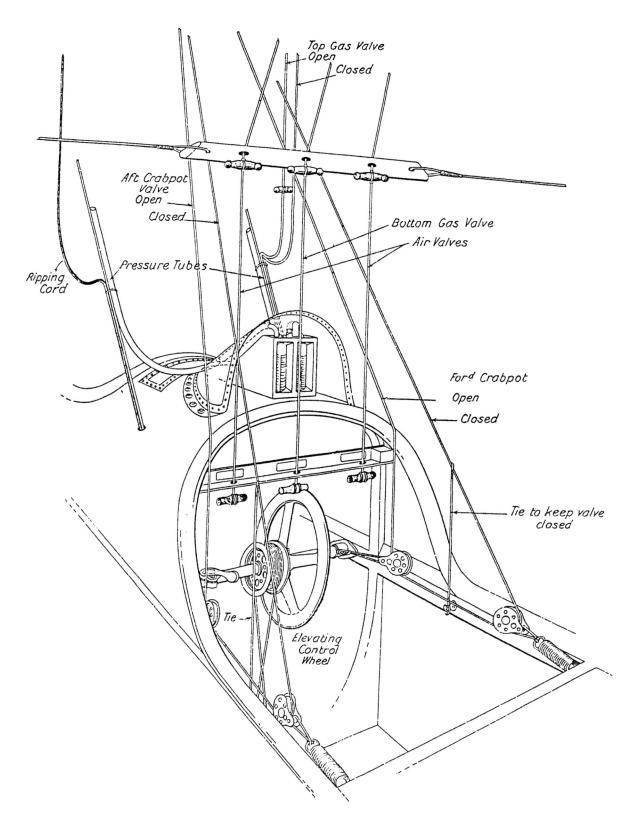

Top Gas Valve
Open
Closed

Aft Crabpot
Valve
Open
Closed

Bottom Gas Valve
Air Valves

Ripping
Cord

Pressure Tubes

Ford Crabpot
Open
Closed

Tie to keep valve
closed

Tie

Elevating
Control
Wheel

25. Most SS airships were controlled from the rear cockpit. The rudder was activated by foot pedals and the elevators by a small wheel. Automatic gas and air release valves were fitted to cope with expansion inside the envelope or the ballonets, but manual control was also provided. Water ballast was contained in a canvas bag, to be released as required, and a few simple instruments were fitted.

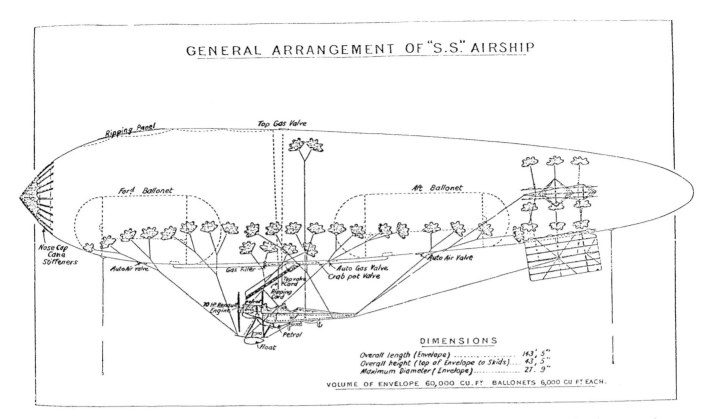

GENERAL ARRANGEMENT OF "S.S." AIRSHIP

Ripping Panel

Top Gas Valve

Ford Ballonet

Aft Ballonet

Nose Cap
Cane
Stiffeners

Auto Air Valve

Gas Filler

Auto Gas Valve
Crab pot Valve

Auto Air Valve

Top valve
cord

Ripping
Cord

70 H.P. Renault
Engine

Petrol

Petrol

Float

DIMENSIONS

Overall length (Envelope) .... 143' 5"
Overall height (top of Envelope to Skids).... 43' 5"
Maximum Diameter (Envelope)................. 27' 9"

VOLUME OF ENVELOPE 60,000 CU.FT BALLONETS 6,000 CU FT EACH.

26. The SS non-rigid blimps had two ballonets placed in tandem. The air was collected from the slipstream by a metal scoop and directed as required through manually operated valves into the ballonets, to maintain the internal pressure and so keep the envelope streamlined. Air could also be admitted selectively to control the trim; favouring one ballonet caused the airship to tilt.

27. The utilisation of the propeller's slipstream to inflate the ballonets was a brilliantly simple solution to one of the main problems of non-rigid airship design. The method was devised for the SS prototype in 1915 and has since been used by nearly all British blimps up to the present day.

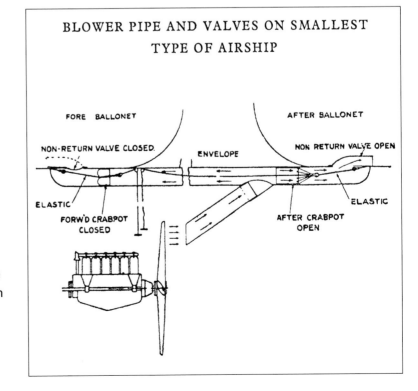

BLOWER PIPE AND VALVES ON SMALLEST TYPE OF AIRSHIP

FORE BALLONET

AFTER BALLONET

NON-RETURN VALVE CLOSED.

ENVELOPE

NON RETURN VALVE OPEN

ELASTIC

ELASTIC

FORW'D CRABPOT
CLOSED

AFTER CRABPOT
OPEN

28. The second type of SS airships was fitted with a Maurice Farman aeroplane car, the engine of which drove a pusher propeller, so enabling the crew to avoid buffeting from the slipstream. These blimps, which were slightly slower than the other two types, used envelopes of either 60,000 or 70,000ft^3 capacity and were usually piloted from the front seat. Seventeen airships of this type were eventually delivered. This photograph was taken on a summer day at Kingsnorth in Kent, where many airships were assembled.

29. SS.13 was built in 1915, but was considered to have an unlucky designation number. Following an accident on the 13th day of the month, she was repaired and renumbered as SS.14A. She was subsequently modified and eventually became the longest-lasting of all British wartime airships, surviving for nearly a year after the Armistice. The twin rudder arrangement was optional on SS airships and gave greater manoeuvrability at the expense of a slightly lower top speed.

30. The third type of SS airships was fitted with an Armstrong-Whitworth aeroplane fuselage as a car and carried the fuel in two cylindrical tanks suspended from either side of the envelope, which was normally of 70,000ft^3 capacity. Each was powered by a 100hp water-cooled Green engine. Sometimes the normal aeroplane undercarriage was retained, but skids or floats were often substituted. Eleven of this type were built, including SS.40.

31. SS.40 was specially fitted with a larger envelope of 83,000ft^3 capacity, which enabled her to reach an operating height of 8,000ft. She was then painted black and loaned to the Army for experimental night-time reconnaissance work on the Western Front during the summer of 1916, so becoming probably the only British airship ever to fly over enemy territory. The results proved disappointing, since she could operate safely only when visibility was poor, and the project was abandoned after two flights. The observer, 2nd Lieutenant C.R. Robbins of the R.F.C. and R.F.A, was the only British soldier to see active service in a dirigible.

32. The SSP or 'Pusher' class of airships appeared early in 1917 and had the advantage of an engine positioned at the rear. They carried a crew of three and saved space in the car by having fuel tanks of rubberized fabric attached to each side of the envelope. Although an improvement on their predecessors, only six were built as they proved inferior to the SSZ or 'Zero' class.

33. The most efficient and numerous of the wartime blimps were those of the SSZ or 'Zero' class, which entered service in 1917. An engineer was added to make a crew of three, and a machine gun – to be fired by the W/T operator – was provided in the forward cockpit for defence. The envelope was of 70,000ft^3 capacity and on each side was slung a petrol tank of aluminium. Altogether, seventy-seven of these blimps were built, of which two were sold to France and two to the United States. They were very popular with their crews and several flew more than a thousand hours in service.

34. The car of SSZ. 27 has a bomb attached to the starboard side and a net with assorted items slung beneath the engine. Unlike earlier blimps, the Zero car was designed specifically for the airship. It was watertight and had a 75hp Rolls-Royce engine mounted on struts at the rear. These features enabled the airship to alight safely on the sea. SSZ. 27 was commissioned in February 1918 and flew 782 hours in service.

35. Airships were faster than surface vessels and commanded a much wider view. Their armament included only a small load of bombs, but if a U-boat was spotted, destroyers or other warships were called up by wireless telegraphy or by Aldis signalling lamp to attack with bombs or depth charges. Here, SSZ. 37 is patrolling with PC.61, a patrol boat designed to look like a small merchant vessel. Both were based at Pembroke.

37. Airships of the Great War relied entirely on vision for finding German U-boats. The submarines used electric motors when submerged and so became vulnerable when they surfaced in order to recharge their batteries. In northern waters they could not be seen at any great depth when submerged, but there were sometimes oil patches or other signs to indicate their presence. When moving just below the surface, the periscope made an inconspicuous but distinctive 'feather' which often betrayed their position.

36. On 7 December 1917, SSZ.16 spotted a surfaced submarine, about a mile away. Uncertain whether it was friend or foe, the airship called by wireless for help and approached cautiously. Suddenly the U-boat's gun opened fire, narrowly missing the airship, which at once raced in to the attack, shooting with her Lewis gun at the sailors scrambling to get below deck. As the submarine dived for safety, bombs were dropped and calcium flares left to mark the position for the destroyers belatedly arriving with depth charges . This is an imaginative reconstruction of the incident by an unknown artist.

38. This contemporary drawing, by Algernon Black, shows airships on convoy duty. In reality, airships escorting convoys usually maintained station to windward. This enabled them to reach any threatened vessel very quickly, instead of having to claw their way slowly back against the wind. So effective was the protection and deterrence provided by the airships, that on only one occasion in the war was a British ship sunk by a U-boat while being so escorted.

39. Signs of a submarine or torpedo could be seen more readily by an airship observer high in the air than by sailors on a ship's deck, looking out at almost sea level. Here a Coastal airship is patrolling in company with a warship.

40. To prevent damage being caused by wind, a large ground crew was usually required when an airship took off or landed, to bring her safely into or out of the hangar. Here, SSZ.3 is being 'walked out' in calm conditions, while a Coastal airship flies overhead. Radially positioned canes prevented the nose of the envelope from buckling at speed.

41. Because of their slow rate of climb, the aeroplanes defending British cities frequently had difficulty reaching the attacking zeppelins. One attempt to overcome this problem was the 'airship-plane' or AP.1. This consisted of a complete B.E.2c aeroplane slung beneath a simple envelope, so making – in effect – an airship with wings that could speedily climb to the desired altitude and then discard the gasbag before going into action. The first trial showed promise, but during the second, in February 1916, the rigging broke, the controls failed and the aircraft crashed, killing its two inventors.

42. The SST or 'Twin' class of airship were the last and best of their kind, but they appeared towards the end of the war and only thirteen were completed, although more than a hundred had been originally planned. Each had an envelope of 100,000ft^3 capacity, a crew of four or five, and two engines to give greater reliability. They could reach 57mph and remain airborne for more than two days.

43. A large handling party was required every time an airship began or concluded a flight, and the stronger the wind, the more men were required. This is an impression of one such occasion, by S. Ugo, a contemporary French artist, where the details of the Coastal airship and its handling ropes are depicted rather more dramatically than accurately. In reality, most airships were provided with a single, long 'trail rope' and several much smaller 'handling guys'. The former was used by the landing party to pull the airship down nearly to the ground, when the latter were seized, the car grasped and the airship manhandled into the hangar.

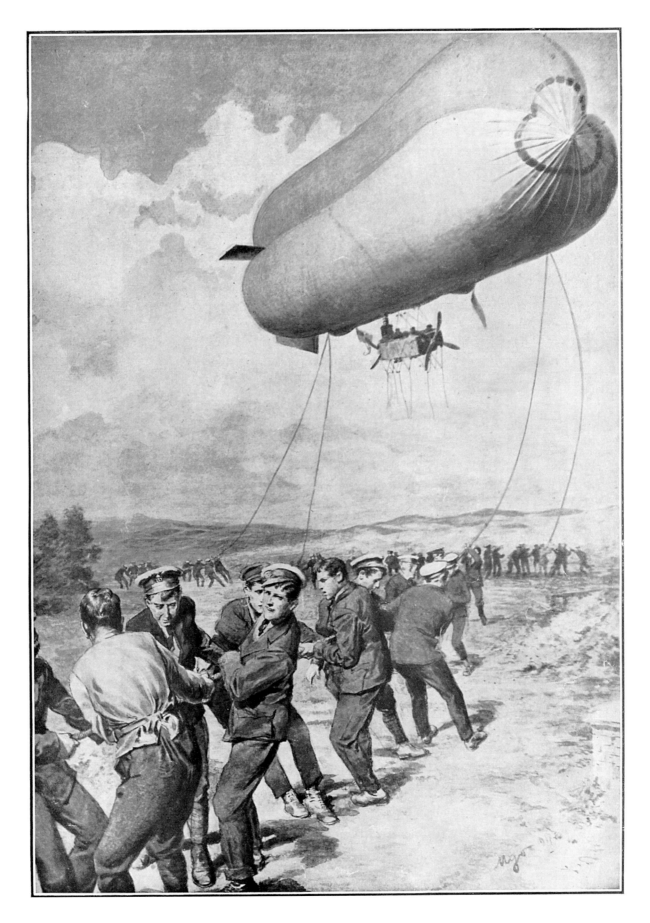

46. The most famous of British wartime airships was C.9. She made her first flight from Mullion, in Cornwall, on 1 July 1916, and flew a record 2,500 hours 11 minutes and an estimated 68,201 miles in service before being deleted from the active list on 1 October 1918. She patrolled the English Channel in all weathers and was often riskily flown without ballast, in order to carry more fuel and bombs. She was involved in many dramatic incidents and on several occasions successfully attacked German U-boats.

47. Flight Lieutenant – later Major – James Struthers was the captain of C.9 during the greater part of her career. He was the most successful of all the British wartime airship commanders and was awarded the DSC and two bars for attacking and sinking enemy submarines. He later transferred to NS.6 at Longside in Scotland and was awarded the AFC.

48. Only two British airships were destroyed due to enemy action during the entire war. These were the Coastals, C.17 and C.27. Both were shot down by German aeroplanes when they strayed too close to enemy-occupied territory. In neither case were there any survivors. British airships were normally safe from air attack, as they usually flew beyond the range of land-based aeroplanes and no zeppelins were ever sent to intercept them. This photograph shows C.23A, a replacement for C.23 and the last Coastal built.

Right: A Coastal airship is brought out of the hangar at Pulham in windy conditions.

49. The Coastal airships were followed by the improved airships of the 'C Star' class. These had a length of 207ft (increased to 217ft from C*4 onwards), a maximum diameter of 47ft and a capacity of 210,000ft^3. They were more streamlined than their predecessors and had a faster top speed of about 57mph. The main fuel tanks were suspended inside the envelope, which was fitted with six ballonets, to improve control.

50. The prototype C Star car was taken from a Coastal, C.12, covered with plywood instead of fabric and improved by the provision of portholes of Triplex glass. Ten C Star airships were built during 1918, all of which survived to the Armistice. The longest recorded flight was of 34 hours, 30 minutes by C*4, commanded by Captain Cleary, on 27/28 May 1918.

51. The 'North Sea' class were the most efficient of the British blimps and were exceeded in size only by the Parseval airships, built by Vickers. The North Sea airships were based on the Astra-Torres design, and each was 260ft long, with a maximum diameter of 57ft, a capacity of 360,000ft^3 and a useful lift of 3.8 tons. They were powered by two engines placed side by side: at first 250hp Rolls Royce, then later 240hp Fiat. Production was cut short by the Armistice, but altogether fourteen airships of this class were eventually delivered, of which one was sold to the United States.

52. The North Sea airships possessed great endurance and carried two crews, together with hammocks and cooking arrangements, in order to enable long patrols to be made. In February 1919, NS.11, commanded by Captain Warneford, set a world endurance record by remaining aloft for 100 hours 50 minutes. On 15 July, the airship exploded in the air off the Norfolk coast near Cley, killing all her crew, after possibly having been struck by lightning. This illustration, from a painting by Nick Walmsley, shows the airship a few minutes before the disaster.

53. The North Sea airships had two cars, although in a few cases these were enclosed together to form one unit. The cars were connected by a wooden gangway supported by cables and sometimes protected by a canvas cover. The rear car held the engines, while the forward car consisted of an enclosed control-cabin behind which were sleeping quarters. Cooking was carried out using the heat from the engine exhausts.

54. NS.7 and NS.8 were both stationed at East Fortune, on the Firth of Forth, during the latter part of the war. On the nearer airship, crew members may be seen on the gangway connecting the forward and after cars. In November 1918, both these airships escorted the German fleet as it came in to surrender at Rosyth. NS.7 became also the last survivor of the wartime airships, making her final flight as late as October 1920.

55. Naval Airship No.4, a German-built Parseval, was bought by the Admiralty before the war and three slightly modified and enlarged versions were later made by Vickers. These were No.5, No.6 – shown here – and No.7 and they were the largest non-rigids ever built in Britain. Each was 301ft long and had a capacity of 364,000ft³. The suspension wires from the car were attached to the envelope by 'trajectory rigging bands', which helped to keep the envelope in shape without the need for excessive internal pressure.

56. The car of No.6 was made of duralumin, with triplex windows, and contained two 180hp Maybach engines driving swivelling propellers. No.6 had a top speed of about 45mph and her large ballonets enabled her safely to reach a height of about 10,000 ft. She flew 406 hours in service and survived for nearly four years before being deleted in October 1919. She was stationed at Howden, in Yorkshire, where she was known to everyone as P.6 or – in acknowledgement of her German ancestry -as 'The zeppelin'!

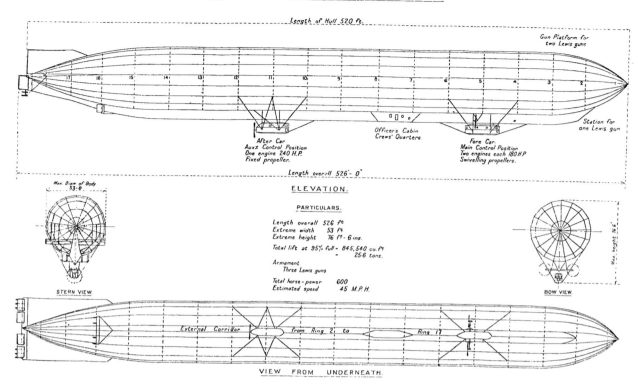

57. The first British wartime rigid airship was No.9, a slow, heavy aircraft that compared very unfavourably with contemporary German designs. She was 526ft long overall, with a diameter of 53ft and a capacity of 846,000ft³. Her framework of light duralumin girders contained seventeen separate gasbags and an internal keel corridor, which widened out to provide crew accommodation amidships. Two cars carried four engines, later reduced to three.

58. Even after intensive lightening, No.9 had a useful lift of only 3.8 tons – the same as a North Sea class blimp – for crew, ballast, fuel and bombs. Her top speed was 43mph and she handled very sluggishly. She was built by Vickers but her design had been largely copied from that of an early zeppelin which had landed in France before the war. Despite being originally ordered in June 1913, she was not delivered until April 1917, when she was already virtually obsolete.

59. Wing Commander E.A.D. Masterman, the senior officer of the Airship Service until April 1918, is at the window of the forward car of No.9. She was captained usually by Flight Lieutenant G.H. Scott and was employed mainly in training and experimental work. However, one uneventful operational patrol was carried out over the North Sea in July 1917, when she covered 404 miles in 26 hours 45 minutes. She was deleted and scrapped in June 1918 after flying 198 hours in service.

60. There were four airships in the 23 class: No.23 – shown here – No.24, No.25 and R.26. In effect, these were modified copies of No.9, with an extra bay and gasbag inserted, three cars fitted and the tail surfaces simplified. One engine was placed in each of the forward and after cars, and two in the midship car. The first three airships were delivered in late 1917 and the fourth in early 1918, but all had to be lightened substantially before acceptance. They were used mainly for training, patrols and convoy duties, but proved to be only slightly more efficient than their predecessor. All four were deleted in 1919.

61. No. 23 was fitted experimentally with a two-pounder gun, mounted on the hull and intended to provide protection against possible attack from zeppelins. The nearby outlets for discharged hydrogen were placed lower down on either side, in order to avoid fire from the gun igniting any escaping gas. In the event, the gun was too heavy to be retained, but no zeppelin was ever encountered by any British airship.

62. No.23 was used for various experiments, including that of carrying an aeroplane for defence against aerial attack. In 1918, a Sopwith Camel was attached below the hull by special fittings and released during flight. The aeroplane flew off successfully, but had to return to base on its own, as no provision was made for retrieval. In later years R.33 was also employed for such trials, but used an improved method which allowed the aeroplane to return to the airship.

63. Most wartime airships took carrier pigeons, for use if the wireless transmitter failed. Here, Captain Little releases a bird through a window in the keel of No.23. A submarine identification chart is on the wall behind him.

64. R.26 was the first rigid airship to be allocated the prefix R. Like other ships of the 23 class, she was 535ft long, with a capacity of 942,000ft^3, a useful lift of 6.5 tons and a top speed of 54mph. She was used for convoy duties and patrols, but saw no action. In December 1917, she flew over London in daylight as a morale-boosting exercise. Like her sister ships, she cost some £125,000.

65. There were originally to have been four ships of the 23X class, numbered R.27 to R.30, but the orders for R.28 and R.30 were cancelled. Of the remaining two, R.27 was destroyed in an accidental fire, but R.29 proved to be the best of the wartime rigids and was the only one to see action. In September 1918, she was on convoy duty near Newbiggin Point when her crew saw a suspicious oil patch on the ocean surface. The airship dropped bombs and signalled by Aldis lamp to the escorting destroyers, which raced to join in the attack with bombs and depth charges. Large amounts of oil flooded to the surface and a U-boat was later confirmed sunk.

66. The control car of R.29 was made of duralumin girders and sheeting. The forward engine drove two propellers, which swivelled as required to raise or lower the airship. The rear car was similarly powered and equipped but at first the car amidships had two engines, each of which drove its own propeller mounted on a fixed bracket to one side.

67. R.29 was 539ft long, with a capacity of 940,000ft^3. She differed from airships of the 23 class mainly in having no keel corridor beneath the hull. This modification made her both lighter and more manoeuvrable. For most of her career, she had four engines, but after the war the two in the midship car were replaced by one in a lighter car and driving a single propeller, as shown here. R.29 was deleted in October 1919, having flown a total of 438 hours and 11,334 miles in service.

68. R.31 was the largest of all the wartime airships. She and her post-war sister ship, R.32, were based on German Schutte-Lanz practice and had hull frameworks made of wood, instead of the usual duralumin. They were each 615ft long with a capacity of 1,500,000ft^3. R.31 originally had six engines, each in its own car, and reached a speed of 70mph during early trials, but one engine was removed before delivery, to increase the useful lift to 19.5 twenty tons.

69. After the removal of one engine, R.31 still had an exceptional top speed of 65mph. She was delivered a few days before the Armistice and flew to Howden, where she remained confined to a hangar until her hull framework fell to pieces due to faulty construction and damp. Her sister ship, R.32, was more successful; she was completed in 1919 and survived until 1921, mainly being used to train American airmen. The two ships were the first in Britain to have a separate control cabin built directly on to the hull and without an attached engine compartment.

70. Large hangars, around a furlong in length, of metal construction and provided with sliding doors, had to be constructed at short notice in several places. The hangar at Pulham in Norfolk cost £150,000 and in July 1919 was able to hold both R.33 and R.34 side by side, each 643ft long and 92ft high. In 1928, to house R.100, it was dismantled and reassembled alongside the hangar at Cardington, where the two still stand today.

71. Airships were frequently damaged when being handled on the ground, and were particularly vulnerable when being taken in or out of a hangar. To provide protection from gusts, large windscreens were often used, as here at East Fortune. Overhead, an early SS airship is coming in to land.

Triumph and Tragedy
1919–1930

In April 1918, the men of the Airship Service became members of the new Royal Air Force, although the Admiralty retained ownership of the airships themselves until October 1919, when they were handed over to the Air Ministry and their numbers reduced drastically, in the interests of economy. Very soon, the Airship Service was closed down altogether and the last surviving airships were registered as civil aircraft. There were many ambitious plans for the commercial use of airships, but these were abandoned temporarily after the R.38 tragedy and permanently after that of R.101. Germany persevered with rigid airships for somewhat longer, while the United States continued to build and fly small non-rigids throughout the Second World War and up to the present day, secure in her monopoly of helium production. In England, as elsewhere, development ceased almost entirely for a generation.

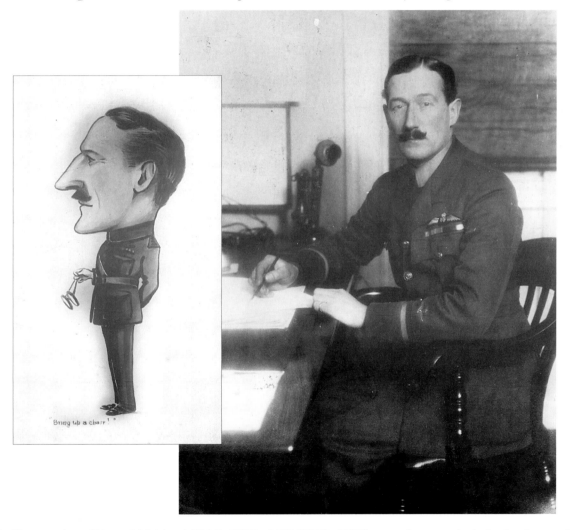

72. Air Commodore Edward Maitland CMG, DSO, AFC (1880–1921) served successively in the Army, the Navy and the Royal Air Force and was the senior British airship officer at the end of the war. Several years earlier he had become the first man to parachute from an airship and he was also a famous balloonist who had flown to Russia in 1908. He was a strong proponent of the rigid airship, in peace as well as in war, and he travelled to America with R.34 in July 1919. He was killed in the R.38 disaster of August 1921. Cartoon from author's collection.

73. A rigid airship under construction. The framework of the hull was constructed of lightweight girders of triangular cross-section. These consisted of running members of narrow duralumin channel braced by diagonals. The whole structure, containing the separate gasbags, was braced by wires and covered by an outer cover of doped linen. The gasbags were inserted and partly inflated during construction. They were made of rubberised cotton fabric, lined with goldbeater's skins. A typical rigid, such as R.34, required some 600,000 skins, from as many animals.

74. R.34 was probably the most famous of all British airships. She was 643ft long, 79ft in diameter and 92ft high. Her nineteen gasbags had a total capacity of 1,950,000ft^3, which gave her a gross lift of some 59 tons and a useful lift of nearly 25 tons. She had five 250hp Sunbeam engines, two of which were geared together to drive a single propeller in the after car. These gave her a cruising speed of about 45mph and a top speed of around 56mph. Her design was based on that of a captured German zeppelin, L.33, and she was built by the firm of William Beardmore in Glasgow. She is shown here at Mineola, New York.

75. In July 1919, R.34 flew from East Fortune in Scotland to New York in 108 hours 12 minutes, a world endurance record. She then flew back to Pulham – as shown here – in Norfolk in 75 hours 3 minutes, having accomplished the first east-west crossing of the Atlantic by air, the first double crossing and the first direct flight between the United Kingdom and the United States. Not until 1933 did an aeroplane equal this last feat. R.34 was destroyed at her Howden moorings in January 1921, by severe winds.

76. The after car of R.34 originally contained duplicated controls, including steering and elevator wheels, for use in an emergency. The latter can be seen through the small window. Here, outside the Beardmore factory, the airship is being 'ballasted up', prior to flight, as the lift is adjusted by adding or removing ballast. The car has been 'eased up' on the ropes of the handling party and the amount of lift is being assessed by finding how many men, holding directly onto the handling rail, are needed to pull the airship down.

77. The crew of R.34:
Back row: Powell Gray Watson Thirlwall Mort Northeast Heath
Standing: Edwards Cross Graham Scull Gent Mays Ripley Robinson Forteath Browdie
Seated: Shotter Greenland Lansdowne Scott Cooke Harris Luck
On ground: Smith Parker Evenden Burgess

There is apparently no extant photograph which shows every member of the crew which flew the Atlantic from east to west. Three officers and one aircraftman are missing here and Heath was not finally selected. Nearly all are still wearing R.N.A.S. uniforms, more than a year after the Airship Service had been officially taken over by the R.A.F.

78. A contemporary artist's drawing of the control cabin of R.34, which was slightly less than 6ft wide. The steering and elevator wheels are to the right, the engine telegraph and the toggles controlling the gas valves and emergency water ballast are to the left. The navigator's table is in the foreground and various instruments can be seen.

79. Apart from R.34, the only other airship in the same class was R.33. She first flew in 1919 and lasted until 1928, so becoming the longest-lasting of all the early British airships. After the closing down of the Airship Service, she was still flown by the Royal Air Force, but registered as a civil aircraft and used mainly for research and training purposes. One experiment involved the release and retrieval of a fighter aeroplane in trials similar to those carried out earlier with No.23.

80. R.33 was provided with two machine-gun platforms, one at the extreme tail – shown here – and one on top of the hull just above the forward car. Both were reached from below by rope ladders in canvas tunnels. It was customary, even during flight, for riggers to walk from one platform to another, along the top of the hull, in order to inspect the outer cover and the gas outlets.

83. R.38 was in her time the world's largest airship, being 699ft long, 86ft in diameter and with a capacity of 2,750,000ft^3. She was to have been sold to the United States and flown across the Atlantic, but she was badly designed and her hull framework could not withstand the stresses of manoeuvring at low altitudes. On 24 August 1921, she broke in two during a turn on her last trial flight and fell into the Humber in flames, killing 44 of the 49 men on board.

84. On 16 April 1925, a fierce storm broke the Pulham mooring mast, releasing R.33 from her anchorage and badly damaging her bows. With only a skeleton crew aboard, she drifted out across the North Sea and over Holland, but her commander, Flight Lieutenant R. Booth, organised mid-air repairs and refused offers of shelter on the European mainland. After nearly thirty hours, the airship managed to struggle back to Pulham and safety.

85. R.101 had many new and untried features. She was found to lack lift and so she was rebuilt with an extra bay, to increase her length from 732ft to 777ft and her capacity from 5,000,000 to 5,500,000ft^3. Despite these and other modifications, she remained too heavy, her engines lacked power and her gasbags leaked badly. Her designers were given no time to correct these faults and R.101 caught fire when she made a forced landing in France on her way to India on 5 October 1930, when 48 of the 54 people on board were burnt to death. This disaster brought an end to airship building in Britain for another generation.

86. The control car of R.101, shown when the airship was under construction in the hangar at Cardington. A 'bumping bag' of compressed air, intended to cushion landing shocks, is fastened beneath and Major G.H. Scott is at the port window.

87. Major George Herbert Scott CBE, AFC (1888–1930) was probably the most famous of all British airship commanders. He was successively captain of airships No.4, No.9 and R.34, which he commanded on the Atlantic flight. After leaving the R.A.F. he was involved with later airship projects and was killed in the R.101 disaster of 1930. Cartoon from author's collection.

88. R.100 was designed by Barnes Wallis and was privately funded, in virtual competition with R.101, which was built with government money. She was 709ft long, with a diameter of 130ft, a capacity of 5,000,000ft³ and a top speed in excess of 80mph. She was the fastest and finest rigid airship ever built in Britain and in 1930, commanded by Squadron Leader R. Booth, she flew without serious incident to Canada and back. Following the R.101 disaster, however, there was widespread disillusion with all airships and R.100 was very soon afterwards grounded and eventually sold for scrap.

89. The AD.1 was the only privately built and owned non-rigid airship produced in Britain between the wars and the only British non-rigid to fly between 1921 and 1951. She was made by the Airship Development Company at Cramlington, near Newcastle, in 1929 and was modelled on the wartime SS class but with a capacity of 60,000ft^3 and a length of 138ft. Intended for advertising, aerial photography and flight tuition, she first flew – oddly enough – on Friday 13 September 1929. She then made several flights, including one over London, before travelling to Belgium to advertise 'Gold Dollar Cigarettes', where she was wrecked in a storm on 7 October 1930.

90. In several places, large masts or towers were erected, from the tops of which airships were tethered by their bows and swung freely like a weather vane, to face into the wind. This method of mooring was intended to obviate the need for airships to be taken into or out of a hangar at the conclusion or commencement of every flight, as this necessitated employing a very large and expensive ground crew. The towers were also usually equipped with lifts and so provided easy access for passengers. This is the tower at Cardington, 195ft high.

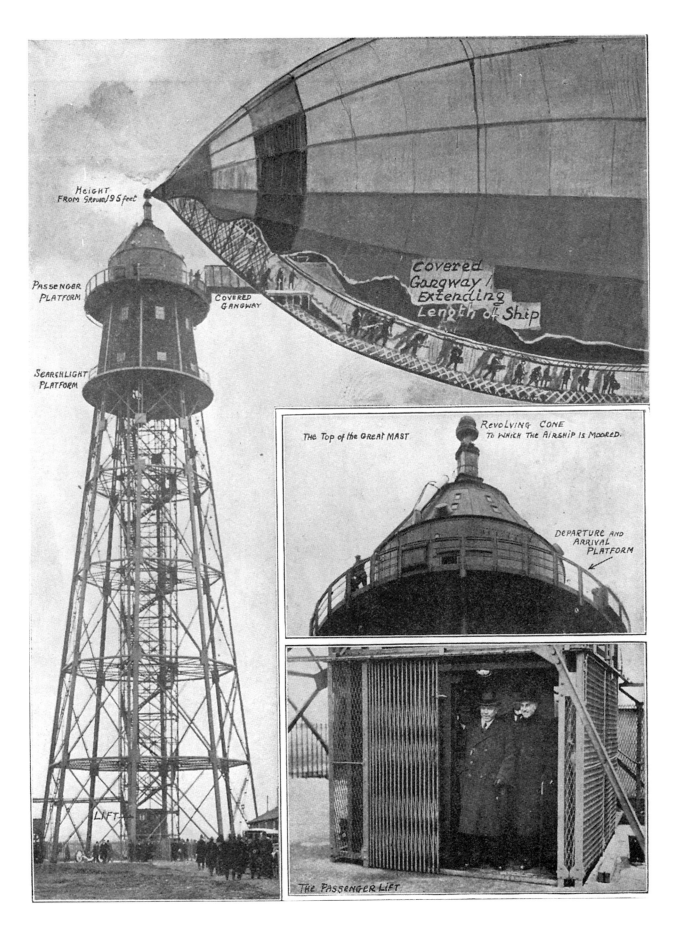

Height From Ground 195 feet

Passenger Platform

Searchlight Platform

Covered Gangway

Covered Gangway Extending Length of Ship

Lift

The Top of the Great Mast

Revolving Cone To which the Airship is Moored.

Departure and Arrival Platform

The Passenger Lift

Demise and Renaissance
1931–1998

After the R.101 disaster, the remaining British rigid, R.100, was soon scrapped, while the only existing non-rigid, AD.1, was wrecked at her moorings. For more than two decades, no native airship appeared in Britain and airship development soon ceased elsewhere in the world, with the one notable exception of the United States. A few private attempts were made to revive interest in airships during the years after the Second World War, but not until nearly half a century after the loss of R.101 was the design and building of airships resumed seriously in Britain and elsewhere in the world. Helium became more readily available and the introduction of propane gas burners allowed smaller airships, as well as balloons, to be inflated with hot-air.

91. In 1951, a group of airship enthusiasts, led by Lord Ventry, built the *Bournemouth*, the first British non-rigid to be flown since 1930. Her envelope was made from an old kite balloon, into which an extra section had been inserted. It was 108ft long, with a diameter of 27ft and a total capacity of 45,000ft³. The car, which was 15ft long, could carry two people, with the pilot forward and the engineer aft, where he controlled the 75hp Salmson engine. The airship flew successfully at Cardington, achieving a cruising speed of about 35 m.p.h., but she proved so expensive to operate that after only eight flights – the last one in 1952 of nearly two hours – she was deflated and stored. All further attempts to return her to service failed for lack of funds.

92. This small airship was built and flown in 1967 by M.A. Brighton, for use in the film *Chitty Chitty Bang Bang*. She was referred to by the characters as a 'zeppelin', but was actually a small replica of a 1904 Lebaudy semi-rigid airship. Her envelope, of rubberised cotton, was 137ft long, had a capacity of 37,000ft^3 and was stiffened by a duralumin keel. She had a wooden gondola to carry two people and her twin propellers were powered by a single 1,200cc Volkswagen engine. She flew only a few times, but achieved fame as the first British airship to use helium, thereafter the universal practice.

93. The Goodyear Corporation of America built *Europa* at Cardington, Bedfordshire, in 1972, using components shipped over from the United States. She was 192ft long with a capacity of 203,000ft^3. and cruised at 35mph with a maximum speed of 50mph. She was used mainly for advertising and publicity, and lasted until 1986, when she crashed in France, but without any of her crew sustaining injury.

95. In 1982, Wren Skyships – later the Advanced Airship Corporation – planned to build large airships with inflexible metal envelopes, rather like the proposed 'aerial ship' of Richard Boyman, a century earlier. These would have combined the separate virtues of the non-rigid and rigid, but none was actually built. This is an artist's impression of the R.40, which was intended to be used by Redcoat Cargo Airlines of Surrey for fast cargo carrying.

94. In 1974, the journalist and author, Anthony Smith, built and flew a small blimp, the *Santos-Dumont*. The use of helium enabled the twin Wankel engines to be fitted close to the envelope, which was short and stubby, with a length of 72ft, a diameter of 28ft and a capacity of 30,000ft^3. The airship was able to reach a speed of 30mph and a height of 5,000ft. She received a Certificate of Airworthiness in 1975 but was eventually taken to America, where the project was abandoned for lack of sponsorship.

96. Airship Industries built several airships between 1979 and 1989, when the parent company failed. The three types produced were the Skyship 500, the slightly larger Skyship 600 and the HL (High Lift) type, which used the smaller type of car but the larger type of envelope. The Skyship 600 shown here was 194ft long with a diameter of 50ft and a capacity of 235,400ft^3. Twin swivelling propellers were fitted to provide vectored thrust and the trim could be varied by differential inflation of the two ballonets, which were fed from the slipstream of the propellers.

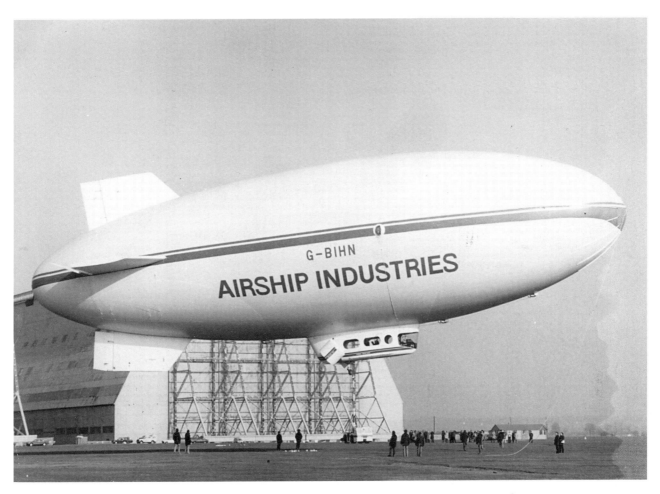

97. The Skyship 500 was 170ft long with a diameter of 46ft and a capacity of 182,000ft^3. Skyship dirigibles were used for tourist flights, fishery patrols, aerial photography and many other duties. For publicity purposes, they were provided with advertising livery consisting of interchangeable banners fastened to the envelope.

Overleaf

98. A Skyship 500 flies over New York harbour and circles the Statue of Liberty.

99. As with all the craft built by Airship Industries, the car was of monocoque structure, built from reinforced plastic, attached directly to the lower surface of the envelope and supported by internal rigging lines. The envelope material was laminated, lined with a gas-retention film and sprayed externally with a polyurethane coating. Passenger accommodation was of a very high standard.

100. In the early nineteen-nineties, the Advanced Airship Corporation of Jurby in the Isle of Man designed the ANR (Advanced Non Rigid) airship, but the project was never completed. It was to have been 200ft long with a capacity of 257,000ft^3 and capable of carrying a crew of two and twenty-eight passengers at a maximum speed of 80mph. At more moderate speeds, it would have had an endurance of up to three days. This is a photograph of a model.

101. Thunder and Colt of Shropshire produced small airships to order in the nineteen-eighties, designed by Mats Backlin and Per Lindstrand. The AS series used hot-air but a small, helium airship was also available. This was the GA-42 , which was 90ft long, with a diameter of 30ft and a capacity of 42,000ft^3. It could carry two people at 45mph for up to seven hours.

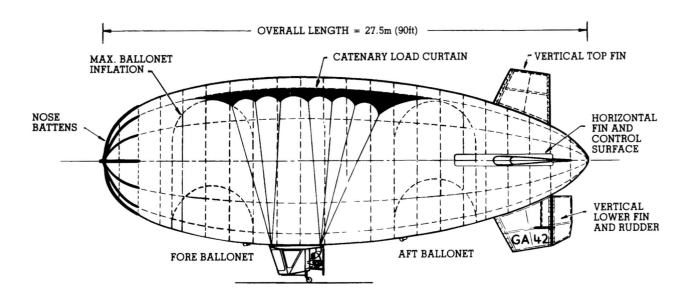

102. The Thunder and Colt AS-261 was in 1989 the world's largest ever hot-air airship, with a length of 150ft and a capacity of 261,000ft^3. It was designed for a botanic survey of the Brazilian rain forest and could carry a crew of five while transporting a three-quarter ton suspended platform. This was placed in position on the forest canopy without damaging the foliage and afterwards retrieved: a task no helicopter or other type of aircraft could have performed.

103. In 1973, Cameron Balloons of Bristol produced the world's first successful hot-air airship. This much later version, the type DP-90, was 115ft long, 42ft wide, 51ft high and had a capacity of 90,000ft^3. It could carry a crew of two.

104. The DG-14 type, designed and built by Cameron Balloons, was the world's smallest ever helium airship. With a length of only 62ft and a capacity of 14,000ft^3, it could be kept in a normal small hangar. It flew at 30mph and cost £70,000 in 1990.

105. The AS-300 was built by Lindstrand Balloons in 1992 as a development of the AS 261, using a new, larger and more efficient envelope, but retaining and improving the existing gondola. In 1993 it became the world's largest ever thermal (hot-air) airship, being 167ft long, with a capacity of 300,000ft^3. Two air vanes behind the pusher propeller could be swung by lever-operated control into the slipstream to act as a thrust reverser, so enabling the airship to brake or go backwards. Other improvements included a new form of catenary load curtain inside the envelope, which eliminated the pitch instability common to its predecessors.

106. During 1997 and 1998, the AT-04 non-rigid airship was being constructed at Cardington. Designed by Roger Munk and the Airship Technologies Group, she will be 269ft long, with a capacity of 501,000ft^3, and be capable of carrying up to fifty passengers in addition to the crew. These figures will make her the largest existing airship in the world, as well as the largest built in Britain since R.101.

Of the engines, two will provide vectored thrust while a third, mounted at the stern, will allow quiet and vibrationless cruising at 53mph when used alone. Together, the three engines will give a top speed of more than 80mph.

This computer simulation shows the wheels partially retracted to reduce air resistance, the bow thruster to improve manoeuvrability and the diagonal arrangement of the tail surfaces.

A provisional list of viable British airships 1902–1998

New airships are being built each year and, even for a fixed time period, it is not possible to make a definitive list of all British airships, since the criteria for inclusion cannot be certain. This list contains only such airships as were recognised, viable or distinct. Excluded are unsuccessful aircraft built before the invention of the internal combustion engine, projects that were not completed and military airships that were built but never officially accepted. British airships sold abroad are included, but not foreign airships purchased from abroad. All are non-rigids except where rigid (r) or semi-rigid (sr) is indicated. All used hydrogen except where helium (he) or hot air (ha) is indicated.

Designation or Description ('Airship' if no other name)	Constructor	Total number	Date first made
Airship	Spencer Brothers	1	1902
Airship	F.A.Barton	1	1905
Willows No.1	Ernest Willows	1	1905
Nulli Secundus No.1	Army Balloon Factory	1	1907
Nulli Secundus No.2 (sr)	Army Balloon Factory	1	1908
Army Airship No.3 *Baby*	Army Balloon Factory	1	1909
Willows No.2	Ernest Willows	1	1909
Army Airship *Beta*	Army Balloon Factory	1	1910
Army Airship *Gamma*	Army Balloon Factory	1	1910
Willows No.3	Ernest Willows	1	1910
Naval Airship No.1 (r)	Vickers	1	1911
Army Airship *Delta*	Army Aircraft Factory	1	1912
Army Airship *Eta*	Royal Aircraft Factory	1	1913
Willows No.4 (Naval No.2)	Ernest Willows	1	1913
Willows No.5	Ernest Willows	1	1913
Airship	Spencer Brothers	1	1913
SS class (B.E.2c car)	Airship Service	29	1915
SS class (Farman car)	Airship Service	17	1915
SS class (Whitworth car)	Airship Service	11	1915
SS class (SS.2)	Airships Ltd.	1	1915
SS class (SS.3)	Short Brothers	1	1915
Parseval class	Vickers	3	1915
Coastal class	Airship Service	35	1916
SS class (non-government)	Vickers	4	1916
No.9 (r)	Vickers	1	1917
SSP class	Airship Service	6	1917

SSZ class	Airship Service	77	1917
North Sea class	Airship Service	14	1917
23 class (r)	Vickers, Beardmore, Armstrong-Whitworth	4	1917
SSE class	Airship Service	3	1918
SST class	Airship Service	13	1918
C Star class	Airship Service	10	1918
23X class (r)	Beardmore, Armstrong-Whitworth	2	1918
31 class (r)	Short Brothers	2	1918
33 class (r)	Armstrong-Whitworth, Beardmore	2	1919
R.80 (r)	Vickers	1	1920
R.36 (r)	Beardmore	1	1921
R.38 (r)	Short Brothers	1	1921
R.100 (r)	Vickers	1	1929
R.101 (r)	Royal Airship Works	1	1929
AD.1	Airship Development Co.	1	1929
Bournemouth	Airship Club	1	1951
Airship (he) (sr)	M. Brighton	1	1967
Europa (he)	Goodyear	1	1972
D type (ha)	Cameron Balloons	35	1973
Santos Dumont (he)	Anthony Smith	1	1974
DS 140 (ha)	Cameron Balloons	1	1976
AD 500 (he)	Airship Development	1	1979
Skyship 600 type (he)	Airship Industries	10	1979
Skyship HL type (he)	Airship Industries	2	1979
Skyship 500 type (he)	Airship Industries	5	1980
AS type (ha)	Thunder and Colt	53	1981
DG 14 type (he)	Cameron Balloons	6	1983
DP type (ha)	Cameron Balloons	30	1986
GA 42 type (he)	Thunder and Colt	6	1987
AS 300 (ha)	Lindstrand Balloons	1	1993
HF 110 type (ha)	Lindstrand Balloons	5	1995

Bibliography

Abbott, Patrick *The British Airship at War 1914-1918,* 1989

Abbott, Patrick *Airship - the story of R.34,* 1973 & 1994

Brooks, Peter W. *Historic Airships,* 1973

Chamberlain, G. *Airships Cardington,* 1984

Clarke, Basil *The History of Airships,* 1961

Davy, M. J. B. *Interpretive History of Flight,* 1948

Gamble, C.F.S. *The Story of a North Sea Air Station,* 1928

Harrison, Michael *Airborne at Kittyhawk,* 1953

Higham, Robin *The British Rigid Airship 1908-1931,* 1962

Jackson, Robert *Airships,* 1971

Jamison, Tom *Icarus over the Humber,* 1994

Jane's *All the World's Aircraft,* 1919

Raleigh, W. & Jones, H.A. *War in the Air,* 1928

Lewis, Peter *British Aircraft 1809-1914,* 1962

Meager, George *My Airship Flights, 1915-1930,* 1970

McKinty, Alec *The Father of British Airships,* 1972

Robinson, Douglas *Giants in the Sky,* 1971

Shute, Nevil *Slide Rule,* 1954

Sinclair, J.A. *Airships in Peace and War,* 1934

Toland, J. *Ships in the Sky,* 1957

Ventry, Lord &

Kolesnik, E.M. *Airship Saga,* 1982

White, William J. *Airships for the Future,* 1976

Acknowledgements

The illustrations in this book come from the following sources (listed by illustration number except where a page is specified):

Airship Heritage Trust: page 6 (top), 9, 10, 14, 15, 16, 17, 18, 19, 20, 23, 28, 29, 31, 32, 33, 34, 35, 37, 41, 42, 52, 55, 56, 58, 59, 60, 62, 63, 64, 65, 66, 68, 69, 70, 74, 79, 80, 81, 82, 85, 88, 89, 91, 93

Airship Technologies: 106

Authors' collections: page 1, page 5, 1, 4, 5, 6, 7, 8, 11, 12, 13, 22, 25, 26, 27, 30, 36, 43, 44, 45, 51, 57, 73, 75, 77, 78, 83, 86, 87, 90, 95, 96, 97, 98, 99, 100

Brighton, M.E.: 92

Cameron Balloons: 103, 104

Fleet Air Arm Museum: page 2, page 6 (bottom), page 8, 46, 47, 48 (bottom), 49, 50, 53, 61

Imperial War Museum: page 4, 24, 38, 40, 48 (top)

Lindstrand, Per: 105

Mechanic's Magazine: 3

Peake, Norman: 21

Royal Aeronautical Society: 72, 76

Science Museum: 2

Scottish Museum of Flight: 39, 54, 67, 71, 84

Smith, Anthony: 94

Thunder & Colt: 101, 102

The authors are grateful for the help they have received from these institutions and individuals. They apologise for any mistakes in attribution which may have arisen due to the frequent presence of identical photographs in more than one archive or to the common difficulty of tracing the original provenance of an illustration.

The authors also wish to thank many others for their help in providing information or guidance. These include Den Burchmore, Giles Camplin, Reg Hillsdon, Mel Kirby, Per Lindstrand and Anthony Smith.